MARCISM TODAY

———————

Marc Mordey

The right of Marc Mordey to be identified as the author of this work has been asserted by him in accordance with the Copyright, Designs and Patents Act, 1988

Copyright ©2013 Marc Mordey

ISBN 978-0-9576791-7-7

All rights reserved. No part of this publication may be reproduced, stored in retrieval system or transmitted in any form or by any means electronic, mechanical, photocopying, recording or otherwise, without the prior permission of the publisher, except in the case of brief quotations embodied in critical articles and reviews.

Published in the United Kingdom in 2013 by Cambria Books, Wales, United Kingdom

Dedications

These poems are dedicated to my mother, June, my grandparents, Ray and Eleanor, and Lizbeth, the family who gave me both roots and wings.

To my sister, Lydia, Dee and Molly.

To my godchildren, Olivia and James.

Especially 'And you Helen', ever my Carningli Queen.

In memory of Vera Neild, Elizabeth Cole, Daphne Auchmuty, Linda Dorrell, Monty Fairfoot, Graham Tuson, Eve Earl, Hettie and Hill Wilson, Ivy and Walter Virgo, Derek Beazley and Clyde Mordey, who have all given me inspiration.

Contents

Introduction	7
My Angels were singing	11
Poet in Motion	15
Alphabet	17
Once	18
Rewarded by Dolphins	20
On Cats and Separation	21
In celebration of Grandparents - Eleanor and Raymond	22
On Carningli in the year 2000	27
Poppies	28
In Kythira, while you sleep	29
Your Heat	30
A Driving along song	31
My Carningli Queen	32
Beating the bounds – 2011	33
September – The Rooks Return	37
Three Word Poem	38
One about hotels	40
One about being at home	41
A hymn to Greece #1 : at Mylopotamos	42
A hymn to Greece #2: Kythira, to be precise	43
And so begins the day	44
Weekend weather report (Tobago)	49
St Francis of Assisi	50
Italy is:	51
Canadian rapture, captured - a song of celebration	55
Catching the No 33	58
Strange Journey	59
A Series of Requiems:	60
Poem for a lost child	60
Lament for Byron	62
A pony for your thoughts	64
Mussels	66
Remembrance Sunday	69
A Confirmation Service	70
England - On the Eve of War	70
Two Rabbits – a poem on 9/11	72
A poem for the Unknown Iraqi	73
Monty's gone	74
For Graham	77
On Grief	78

The Sun	79
Taken from headstones in a Battersea graveyard	80
Springtime	81
September Song (#1) for you	83
September Song (#2) for you	85
Snowfall over Newport	86
Spring driven thing	87
At Sea	88
Epiphany	89
A small poem about weather and feeling angry	90
Lost in translation?	93
What (maybe) God (might) think of the World	95
and finally ... a tongue twister	97

Introduction

When I was about twelve, my English Teacher at Hereford High School for Boys, Mr D Sparks, set us the task of keeping a journal, but very specifically said to me that I was to write my journal as poetry. I will never know why he said that but I thank him for it, for poetry has been my principal method of keeping a note of the people, friendships, situations, views, landscapes, loves and losses that have fuelled my life.

At 6th Form College I attended a reading entitled 'Two Poets in a Bath'. One of the poets was Brian Patten who has been a ceaseless source of inspiration.

During the last years of the 1990's my personal life went through a difficult patch. In 2000 everything changed when I enrolled on a creative writing course in Greece. I left the UK still in a troubled frame of mind, arrived on the magical island of Kythira and fell in love with my tutor, novelist Helen Carey (http://www.helencareybooks.co.uk), who would later become my wife. So, in my view, I came home with the First Prize!

Now living mainly in Pembrokeshire, tucked under Carningli (Mountain of Angels) with views over the Irish Sea, I find plenty of inspiration both from landscape and from life. This collection has emerged as a result of the success of my poetry blog http://themarcistagenda.wordpress.com, named in tongue-in-cheek homage to my University of Cardiff politics degree.

So here is my take on the world and the times we live in. I hope you will find something here that speaks to you, and I thank you, most sincerely, for sharing in my creative adventure.

Marc Mordey

To begin

My Angels were singing

a poem for St David's Day

I stood near the house
where Grace once lived.
My angels were singing.

I watched as birds
and daffodils dived.
My angels were singing.

It's spring and the sun
bursts fat and alive.
And my angels were singing.

Old crow, silhouetted against Carningli rock,
Purple-shadowed on blackened, burnt bracken,
gorse and heather reeling,
in the aftershock.

But my angels were singing still,
as seagulls wheeled across the bay,
catching sea breezes,
tumbling at will.

The Irish Sea lies beneath
becalmed and silvered blue,
and my angels were singing.

Wales' favourite saint remembered,
the new season breaks forth, springing,
flowers dancing, church bells ringing.
His angels singing.

Seasons, people, live and die,
here and now is for the living.
But remember those you love or loved –
do try.
And let your angels be singing.
Let your angels be singing.

Premillenial

Poet in Motion

This poem was written ages ago, 9/6/99 in fact. I was listening to Andrew Motion being interviewed (on BBC4 Today programme I think) just after he had become Poet Laureate, wherein he bemoaned the lack of time.

Such a commotion,
the very notion,
"no time to smell the roses,"
says Mr Motion ...

We are most fraught
at the very thought,
what,
"no time to stop and stare?"
It's enough to make any literary critic
lose their equilibrium,
if not their hair.
We need our Laureate
to contemplate
and ruminate,
to lyricise,
to amble
to dawdle,
and to gently criticise.
To set the world to verse,

with time allowed for reflection,
for meditation upon our mutual direction ...

So please Mr Poet Laureate,
no rush,
but lots of shush,
indeed, more hush,
for, as one supposes,
the job of poet
can only be,
to take time to smell the roses.

Alphabet

Aching
Ball breaking, busted up
Coping – I think
Defining (moments)
Enervating, excruciating
Frustrating
Grieving
Heaviness of heart, horizons fractured
Irrationality, irritability – in pain
Jollity (false, on the whole)
Kissing – wish I was – keeping on
Limbo, love and the loss thereof
Misery, melancholy, mourning
Nil desperandum – easily said
Ordinary life continuing, yet your world has stopped, incredibly so
Poverty of spirit
Questioning, querulous, quack – you're all ducked up
Remembering, rationalising, revisiting, revising history
Sobbing, stifling, so, so sorry
Talking (tough), tentative steps forward
Unwilling – to "snap out of it"
Vacating (erstwhile home) vacuum, volatile
Wanting, wakeful, wishing, walking, wistful
Zero – "everything is less than zero"

Once

Once, we knew the minutiae of one another's lives,
Lived within inches of each other
Shared intimacies, emotions much more besides
Meals, movies, music and friendships
Cats and the garden
Summer-housed evenings, cigars and beers
Galleries and cafes
Department stores and DIY
Conversation and companionship
Once.

Then
Somehow
I don't know how
The differences
Cherished and consistent
Became distances
Calamitous and cataclysmic.

Then
I watched us move apart
Stared across the chasm
But could not shout, scream, speak
"Beware! Our love might just fall
Down there!"

Now
I know fragments only
Of how you live
Snippets of news from friends
And brief meetings
Tidying up our own loose ends
We are a million mile asunder.

I turn away
Embrace the counsel of despair
Yet also allow myself to begin to wonder
If my journey will lead me elsewhere?

Rewarded by Dolphins

And what does a birthday bring?
A child being sick, before we even leave the harbour
(making my breakfast somewhat uneasy!)
a memory of Ireland,
old faces, and ancient places,
ice cream and cold Guinness,
and a beach, thick with shells
drummed by racing horses -
beyond the beach where Jackie stayed
after they stole her Jack away.
And what does a birthday bring?
Cold hands in a strengthening wind,
and seabirds coasting the breakneck waves.
And I've a new, blue hat.
And five, yes five, dolphins, breaking out of the blue.
Leaping, skimming and arching,
spelling out something new to come.
And I am rewarded by dolphins.

On Cats and Separation

Two cats
captured in mock bronze,
neither cheap
nor tawdry
"an approximation of the Real McCoy"
you once stated.
Of the divine Rosie and Malika
who smelled of hot fur,
straw from the cattery,
vile food
and, occasionally,
grass and vomit!
Their vitality,
their lithe writhings
were
oh
so
real.

This statue, this mocking bronze,
cast
amongst myriad memories
of you,
smells now of nothing.
Not even the desolation
I once managed to attribute to it.

In celebration of Grandparents - Eleanor and Raymond

A couple of pieces that relate to my grandparents, who I loved dearly, and who gave me an inspirational vision of what ageing well can be like – a path made much easier for them by my mother, who made sure that their long journey was a comfortable and an honoured one.
"Ray and Nellie" were married for just over 70 years.

UNTITLED

Thinking of you,
grandfather, my love,
blue bearded and green pyjamad
as you lay, serene in death.
What were you thinking of in those last, feather breathed days?
Of beer, and skittles?
Old cars and older friends?

Loose fittings, loose ends?
Or was it of us, or had you already left us behind, pretty much as we suspected, our solicitations rejected?

I like to think that some image of us, your loves,
was imprinted upon your mind's eye
as you slipped out of the room
with one final, short sigh …

My grandmother (the angel on my shoulder) died about 18 months after Ray and as part of the eulogy for her funeral service I wrote:

When I travelled to France recently, on the overnight ferry, towards midnight I went out on one of the upper decks. The moon was rising and romancing the sea, and I had the strongest sense of my grandfather, heard him talking to me, and felt his presence. And I imagined him dancing a ragged and solitary hornpipe atop the silvered waves. (And then, because I am his grandson, I went and had a coffee and a cognac, and chided myself for being whimsical.)

Well, I like to think that the same moon-spangled carpet will be laid out across the sea tonight, and, if I was making my voyage again, that I would see the sailor and the lady, sitting at a table, straight backed and forever young. For an instant they might look towards my ghost ship passing by, and, later, I think they will turn and look eagerly for us all.

But for now? They only have eyes for each other.

Postmillenial

On Carningli in the year 2000

Climbing Carningli
I walked behind you,
Admiring your long body.
Sharing a little of your past,
Hoping for a place in your future.
I saw no angels,
Though we had glimpsed demons the night before,
Curtained by hot salty tears.
Carningli's spirit blew them away.

At the top of the mountain
I sat in silence
And allowed my thoughts to peak.

Descending, I did not make a wish,
Oh well,
I will hold it in reserve.
But if I did, it would be
That you, that I,
That we all,
Receive the love
That we deserve.

Poppies

The poppies in Lorna's wall
Can grow on from almost nothing
And split the sky asunder,
Fat red petals and red flushed beauty.

Us?

We grow on a rich loam, shared earth,
Great joy and the sense of wonder.
Of course, it cannot always be Kythira,
But ever Aphrodite's promise:
"Love, over duty."

In Kythira, while you sleep

Once more, you sleep
As the honeyed skies of Kythira keep
Watch over you.
As do I.
The lingering taste of grapes upon my breath,
The gentle curve of the steepening wind
Whistles the olive groves into silvered stealth.
The small sounds of a bucket
Beaten to the ground.
Birdsong.
A cockerel crows.
The gregarious greetings of the soft eared hound.
You lie marined in your blue head band,
Muted breaths, the occasional twist or turn
Marring your otherwise perfect sleep.

And the tiny wind spun angels of Kalamos keep
A watch over you,
Under the dolphin blue Grecian sky.
As do I.
As do I.

Your Heat

Your heat
permeating my sleep,
warming my mornings,
setting alight my dreamings,
the dreams that keep
revisiting and returning
even when apart,
your heat
to warm my heart.

Your heat
a hot spot
in the big bed,
drawing me over
"not waving but drowning"
in your heat.
Infinitely preferable
to living in stable,
climate controlled comfort.
Your heat.

A Driving along song

Picturing you,
Whistling up to Oxford in your newly atyred car.
Missing you, willing you to
Be back early.
Life has kept us, and our vehicles, in
A flat spin
This summer gone.
Will the autumn prove more mellow?
I trust that you will allow
Me to help you
As best I can.
The road ahead may not be obvious,
Even harder to see
Through the fog of loss, but
Let's tread it together.
Whilst our course may alter,
Destination, as yet unclear,
My depth of feeling for you
Does not falter,
Simply shifts up another gear.
I don't need a map as such,
Just, perhaps, a guardian angel, a guide.
And to hug, to touch,
To share, to care,
And to travel as closely, side by side,
As we can,
As we dare.

My Carningli Queen

Carningli
Crowns the bay
As I stare hard
On this perfect summer's day
At the blue-green world
Yawning beneath me.
Gasping to the top,
I clasp at stone
And lay a new gift,
A blessing, ordered to complement
My bent-pin, wishing well thoughts,
Atop the gathering cairn.
Rested, renewed,
My legs construed
To return me to you
And your melon scented kisses.
You, the jewel
In my Carningli crown.

Beating the bounds – 2011

First we met amidst the cheerful noise and roar of living,
Squared off in Market Street
The horses shying, nudging nervously,
Eager to avoid lorries, cars, the inconvenient pedestrians.
Saddled up and stirrup cupped, they sally forth, and,
Like some star crossed lovers,
Their paths and the walker's ways are not to cross again, this day.

It's a long road to the end of Long Street,
"And miles to go before we sleep".
The walkers convene, eager to beat, maybe even break the bounds.
For we are living history today and the wildly beating western heart of Wales
Resounds, and steers these wilful feet.
Estuary and sea behind us,
Swiftly we stride the road of kings
Where Henry Tudor once slipped towards
Bosworth on paths of glory,
And, daring to cross the 21st century once more,
We make our way behind, beyond Hendre farm
The leet singing softly across the centuries,
Testament to engineers of another age.

Stepping stones and hawthorn copses, and
For some a speedy detour around
the long deserted, but still upheld,
Stone encircled cattle pound – a mournful story of shillings lost,
Some here before us were to count the cost.

Its uphill now, and the wind is there to whip us lightly,
A few drops of rain to remind us of where we are.
But we are following the flag, in its wind kissed flight.
Resolute, you might say, marching
Towards Bedd Morris, and the standing stone,
Where, for a slither of time and a mouthful of sandwich,
Ennobled by mayor and mayoress, resplendent in red,
We rest, and are thankful;
Apart from one young beaten boy, perhaps,
For his is the freshest mind on show, and, let's
Make no bones about it, if the young are to remember the ancient boundaries,
They must be beaten soundly for their troubles.
"The youth of today" echoes down the years,
As the stick swishes in the stiffening breeze,
But this is pantomime only, photographs and cheers – no tears.

Refreshed, and joined by dogs and other new companions,
Fresh for the journey, but walking age old paths,

The mountain top soaked in colour,
Purple heathered and gorse honeyed
And the red and white of the flag, breaking the blue grey cloud.
Sheep safely graze, though they and skulking foxes, rabbits and a small mountain lizard
Might be forgiven for being a trifle amazed at this unforeseen traffic,
A Carningli crocodile, a human hazard.
We pass the stone circles that once were home to those long lost,
Skirt the side of "Angel Mountain", no celestial voices to be heard,
But the song of the lark arouses, a buzzard cries and wheels above,
Riding the thermals, untroubled by time,
Undaunted by history.
The skies open up before us, the sea and cliffs ahead,
Below, Chapels, Manor, Nevern church
Well mannered fields, undisciplined outcrops and wayward woodland,
Many passed those ways, wrote the tapestry of time,
Though for most our life stories remain unread.
For today, the Pilgrim's Way is above the valleys
And we've time in hand, as downwards, dogs dancing, we are led.

Back to Newport, job done, a stalwart crew,
We salute our standard bearer and make plans to meet

And that evening are rewarded with revelry,
And, later a form of reverence
As the Llwyngwair Arms falls silently to keep watch
Over the time bound tradition, the Court Leet.
Certificated, we walkers, riders too,
Take our place in the boundless tale.

Above us, Carningli sleeps,
Dented by our passing, brushed by our boots, hammered by hoof beat,
The drum and the dragon, magical and mystic, the mountain top steeped in sound.
We, time straitened fragments of history, move forward now, on into our own futures.
But today we made our mark,
And companionship, community, purpose and vigour, these are the features.
Abundant memories, to lighten the winter dark.

September – The Rooks Return

As our Indian summer begins to wane
I walk through the backfields
Of the Eastbury churchyard
Where "And you Helen" Thomas rests.
The stillness of the gravestones
And bowing yew hedges
Broken only by the wing-beat
And harsh, hoarse calls
As the rooks return.

Three Word Poem

Sometimes, when I
am sure that
you are sleeping
deeply, I lie
in the blanketed
calm of the
huge bed we
share and I
whisper the three
word poem against
your strong back,
and let it
traverse your spine
and, I hope,
it then lies
sublime, within your
sub consciousness and
the three words
flutter through to
your lazily sleep
beating heart, so
that, when you
start your new
day, each one
an adventure, I
trust, you will

feel enveloped, protected,
as so you
must, by the
spirit which developed
over these glorious
years, months and
days. And now
my three word
poem, amaze, revel,
cherish, adore and
again, I say
AMAZE!

One about hotels

Upstairs,
In the room above,
The floorboards porcelain thin,
He appears to be
Talking on the telephone.
Phoning home?
It's 3:17 a.m.
There is birdsong too,
Blackbirds,
Confused by lamplight.
At 4:00 a.m.
Someone is padding about
Outside my door.
At 4:40 a.m.
I make tea
A cup of Tranquility
(sweet irony)
My friend, above,
Is snoring deeply.

One about being at home

a contrast to hotel living

Waking
5:30 a.m.
still wishing to drift
fumble minded
back to sleep
our hands
meet
across the duck down folds
of the dawning bed
birds are calling
towards
the now waning moon
we stroke one another
slide together
a human spoon
warmth, safety, security

A hymn to Greece #1 : at Mylopotamos

At Mylopotamos
you swam
brown skinned and blonde hair
cleaving
the deep fissured, blue veined water
and you rose
cleansed of salt and sand
pooling our emotion.
Surely some latter day Aphrodite?
If not
her daughter.

A hymn to Greece #2: Kythira, to be precise

I think
that I could live,
live well
and long,
in a little town
like Livadi
where the Greek coffee
at Rena's café
is strong
and sweet
and where some of the men
of this small town
meet
to chew the fat
as the honey streaked sun
beats them
into the shade

And so begins the day

Somewhere in Namibia
a leopard is lying beneath a tree,
blind-siding us tourists, sometime hunters,
with its leaf dappled camouflage,
and languid torpor,
both disguising energy, inert now
yet readily explosive.
Nearby, cheetahs will be splayed in threesomes
on a red dirt road,
a regally indifferent display.

And so begins the day.
The iron-age redded,
silvered grass, bed spreaded,
yellow mountained, empty fountained day.

At Etosha, the jackals will still be bewilderingly
coated in their dog like innocence,
soft tones concealing a vicious core,
slinking sylph like across the brightly flowered
savannah floor.

And so begins the day.
The wildebeest, kudu, springbok freckled day,
the guinea fowled, goshawked, sandgroused
speckled day,
as ostriches primp and pirouette,
unlikely ballerinas,
silhouetted against the elephant skinned
mountains.

At Doro !Nawas,
the fort like, bush burnt blackened walled cabins
will be staring out at the purple mountain rimmed
canyon calling plains.

And so begins the day.
The eleven elephant trailed, green-grassed and
water-holed,
Egyptian goosed, African shelducked, blacksmith
plovered,
warthog clovered day.

Would that we could have stayed
To watch those desert adapted, brown dirt
slapped
done and dusted, grey skins crusted
matriarch led,
cooling pastures ahead,
marching solemnly on our Namibian parade.

At Erongo,
The sun will already be lingering upon
early morning worship baboons and dassies,
embracing dawn's ritual greeting.
Gentle pinked and yellowed warmth
falling soft and pillowed on precariously placed boulders
is the light and heat of youth, renewal, the beginning;
though throughout the ever baking day
it falls more vengefully
and, like them, like us
it ends the African day, diminished, older.

But, just for now, so begins the day.
The quietly tented, spread eagled mountain valleyed day,
the plumply doved, glossily startling starlinged day
the cuddled dassied, love birded, yellow canaried day.

At Kulala Wilderness Lodge,
even now,
the greened mountain passes are peaked by balloons
and the vlei is buttered by creamy dancing grasses.

A weaver sociably passes by my balconied morning
and sadly for us, this particular dawning
also heralds a return, a parting,
for this day we two take flight,
no worries, we hope, of being predated,
simply put; to be repatriated.

Yet, so, still, begins the day.
The red duned, sharply shadowed, angled and sand sculpted day,
the dancing white lady spidered day,
snake, lizard and jackal tracked day
haring through the dunes,
the film crewed, acacia strewn, desert safaried day
the beetle browed, bemothed and butterflied day.

And we still have the road to Windhoek to adventure
before returning to our own small herd.
African sky emboldened, embedded, enamoured.
Gravel road beaten though largely undeterred.

To leave this place and space
is sad.
And to come here again, would be good.
But travelling home
with lovely you
is to be glad.

And so begins the day.
African adored.
Sunshine stored.
And oh, so very, very glad.

Weekend weather report (Tobago)

Caribbean cock crow morning.
Bananaquits
split the never silent night,
cheeping and chattering
as the deepening dawn sets in.
Alongside the sea,
chocolate milkshake silvered,
sighing onto the beach,
palm trees have shed coconut husks
which lurk, frustratingly beyond surf's reach.
Trumpet trees, mimosa too,
a beady eyed chicken struts past,
dogs and humming birds
have oh! so very much to do.

There's a pink flushed cloud ahead of me
a Barbie dolled sky to cheer
yesterday's rain away
and, monsoon free,
the weekend is left to us,
loud and clear.

St Francis of Assisi

The rain, unexpected and more than a little blissful,
Keeps us in the church of St Francis of Assisi
A while longer than otherwise we might have chosen.
A tiny tiled figure of a blackbird
Graced a flag-stoned tomb.
Gregorian chanting
Seeps softly through the air.
I light a candle for our departed dead,
And feel sure and glad to be alive.
Yet, still, a little wistful.

Italy is:

Sunlight slicing the morning apartment,
Gracing the piazza too,
Streaming over the crimson and cream banners,
Caressing cappuccino coffee cups,
And lighting the way for the young baristas-to-be,
Who are hawking cups of rosemary water,
Whilst bric-à-brac trembles in the spring wind.

It's Antonella's pasta with fennel
And basking in her salted, amber glowing cellar,
Graced by Roberto's gentle, courteous conversation.
It's Crodino, Americano, cat motifs, cornettos,
And Enrica's charming welcome.

It is you and I dozing alongside the Tiber
As it flows greenly by,
Kingfishers calling,
A chestnut cob rolling in a dust bath
Amidst the sylvan spring countryside.
Smoke whisping through the olive groves,
And a farmer raking fresh mown grass.

It is forcing ourselves up vertical cobbled streets,
Sipping lemon soda on a tiny terrace,
Being amazed at the crazed musings and meandering

Of medieval planning.
A Moroccan lamp catching the sunlight
Above a dusty wood bandaged and padlocked door.
Madonnas and St Francis sitting serenely in relief
Above ancient archways.
And it is pistachios purchased in the lee of history.

Italy is lakes and splendour,
Fettuccine and ravioli consumed
High above the water,
Local white wine, honeyed and soft.
The Italian Airforce museum, and
Planes hurled aloft.

It is gambling with hectic traffic in Tivoli,
The mossed water delights of the Villa d'Este,
Intense, green chiselled pleasure gardens.
A bride, beside the Cypress pencilled skyline.
Wild cyclamen, purple flag irises,
Gargoyles, monumental architecture,
Dwarfing statues and confusing the gods.

It is Hadrian's Villa,
The insistent clamour of modernity,
Juxtaposing
The silenced weight of the ages,
Muffling the shadow stained ruins.
Pierced by the delight of children, untroubled by time,
Yet to become their own slight slice of history.
The might of erstwhile empire

Captured by omnipresent electronic aids.
A terrapin floating serenely in the great pool,
No carping about the past there.

Italy is an ice cream diet,
Being woken by words at 5 in the morning,
Grappa fuelled brain stumbling,
An early evening promenade,
A carousel in the park,
Evening's silky silence, punctuated by footballing children
Twisting, tumbling.
The gossip and smoke of their elders,
The riot of oranges, artichokes, tomatoes
Pastries, flatbreads, pizza slices and olives.
Wine stained plastic bottles,
Peroni filled shelves.
Hustling bustling restaurants,
And a woman gently selling Chinese novelties.

Italy is:

The curling call of the hoopoe,
Pining in Farnese woodland.
The sonorous symphony of church bells,
And the threading road
That laces up to the Palazzo,
Cluttered and steeped with mourners,
Gathered, sombre coated and ten rows thick
Though not for that once great family,
Now extinct,

Who left us frescoes and blue gold maps of the world,
The impressions of exploration,
The vulgarity of GPS yet to be discovered.

It's you in new Ray Bans,
Gracing my movie,
Dreaming downstairs.
Giving me,
As only you know how,
La Dolce Vita.

It's life, vigour, the weight of history.
For this one week
It's the street where we live
Carpe Capena,
Pot planted and balconied,
Lamp lit and almond blossomed,
Monastic, mosaiced and modern.

It's the joy of today,
Of spring and of sunshine,
Balanced, cushioned and unclouded.

Italy is - a holiday.

Canadian rapture, captured - a song of celebration

It was our wedding day and
in the moon capped, early morning light,
(the one I love the best,)
I watched you sleep,
your blue bandana streaking your rest.
Pretty in pink
and pillowed breathing.
Wedding day dreaming?
No stags, nor hens, the night preceding,
but two humming birds milked the late night scents.
Later, great horned owls, two again,
ghost winged past us,
a stately proceeding through the pines.
It all made sense,
these avian blessings.
You and I, entwined.

The sunlight cracked the morning mountains,
and on the day, the view
emboldened us once more.
The jagged, lizard spine bowled us over,
bouldered beauty abounded.
Under oath, you took me,
and I you.
And we were proud,
to be so
avowed.
Overhead, two eagles soared,
testimony perhaps?
Promises, destinies, futures,
tried, tested, assured.
Later that day,
waxwings flashed across an emerald coloured lake,
a woodpecker belted out a treetop drumbeat.
We paddled gently, made no mistake
and made a wedding breakfast
in British Colombian heat.

Driving back, Calgary bound,
a pick up truck split the prairie side
streaming a dust dirt cloud.
Bluebird boxes decorated our journey.
We revelled in the wedding day drive,
fulfilled, enriched
and proud.
Time moved on,
birds, holidays, all took flight.

Today
We are in a different place,
but find ourselves
happy, still
fat and full
with
wedding day delight.

Catching the No 33

Some small rebellion took place
in the crocodile of tiny children
winding past me,
a primary school parade.
"Is this the right side for Milton Keynes?"
"Ask Mrs Wheeler, she'll know."
The crocodile placed on hold,
Mrs Wheeler confirms that
it is so.
Meantime, Susan and Darren are told off for
"letting go of your partner."
The command to resume connection is given
crisp, but not unkind.
And the children snake off
into the mornings blinding sun.
Leaving me, cloud breathed alone
waiting on the Number 33
to Milton Keynes.
And I have got
Jimmy Webb's music
running rich and wild
within my veins.

Strange Journey

They travelled
From the Celtic West
Into the flatness of the East
To claim their dead.
Little left,
If anything indeed,
Of what might have been the best.
Instead,
The bitterness of defeat.
Strange journeys,
We all take them,
Yet none so sour,
Nor yet so sweet,
As when our destiny we meet.

Ultimately we are all
Just visitors,
Though who can know
What new vistas we might yet enjoy,
And which friends we might get to greet?

A Series of Requiems:

Poem for a lost child

Grief is cast upon the midnight water
Of Aphrodite's Pool.
No more to mourn for our son – or daughter.
Their heat,
Once redly bright within you,
Is now a starlight, milky cool.

The fragrance of three sweet jasmine flowers,
To mingle with salt lick spray,
Must bear away these latter, anguished hours,
Our child has had its longest day.

And two hollyhocks,
One White,
One Red,
Will cheer us through
This shortest night.

And, as the aftershocks of loss diminish,
And what we began,
We learn to finish,
May we be granted second sight,
To know that life is still so precious, so pure,
And what we have, who we hold,
One another,
Can only be
So very right.

Lament for Byron

Always called me 'bach' you did,
Asked for Helen, Rosemary, the pony too.
Knew all and everyone you did,
No ignoring folks for you.
Rumbled down the lane on your vintage tractor,
Always the offer of a trailer,
A helping hand.
Stewarded friend's houses,
Bought ponies with Derek,
Laid water pipes,
Upturned baths for thirsty creatures,
Understood this land.
Knew Newport and cared for it too.
Hobnobbed with the Lady Marcher,
Presided over the Court Leet,
The Town Council.
Always generous with the meet and greet.
Bothered about it all, and us,
Did you.

Your passing leaves us diminished.
A certain wisdom finished.
A mighty memory
Underscored.

Resplendent, red robed
And not to be ignored.
We made you Mayor,

High praise indeed, but, really,
You should have been
A Lord.

A pony for your thoughts

No need now to leopard crawl around the kitchen
Whilst making breakfast tea
Trying to avoid your scrutiny and strident summons.
No longer the ritual of twice daily feeds,
The sweet smell of pony nuts and alfalfa,
The dusty musk of hay,
The quickening clip up the field as you hurried for your commons,
The chopping of bulk bought carrots.
No more satisfying your imperious demands and needs.
No need now to stifle the taste of medicines
In a black treacle sugar bomb.
No call for grooming, for brush, for curry comb.
Who will keep the pheasant company now?
How will magpies gather horse hair for their nest?

Gone, the gentle push of mossy muzzle,
The warm whickers at the gate,
The chance to chat to you in your shelter,
To even practice salsa dance steps (to your surprise),
To witness sunset, sunrise
And the twilight thrills of these star dark skies.
Gone the fearsome rat stamping hooves,
The pony roll amongst spring grass and orchids,
The occasional frantic field wide gallop,

One eye always on the five bar gate,
Ever ready for escape.
Yesterday, I found you mounded,
Fallen, your body a still living boulder
But collapsed on the brackened, brambled floor.

Blanketed, soothed, then sedated,
I stroked your face as you nickered,
Panicked, wheezed and rattled,
Then calmed, relaxed, got settled.

The vet came, and sent you peace ward.
And now we'll go a waltzing with Matilda
No more.

Mussels

Two mussel shells lie symmetrically
sand splittingly
emptied, purpled,
no longer purposeful, nor poised,
but still eye catching,
even artistic.

We went rock pooling with George and Anna,
fish-nets, buckets, a camera that could fall underwater,
remaining breathless, but unabashed.
A host of crabs, deceased.

Newport Bay
splendid in this first flush of summer.
June, bursting out all over
(a tune to annoy my mother).
The rock pools, hissing and popping,
liquid delight,
sea fronds lapping,
sea weed slurping the soupy dents
of time blackened rock.
Urchins below,
scallywags and dogs above.

And a pirate cave beyond
towards Morfa Head,
the sea soporific in milky stillness
and a thrifted cove yawning in unison.

So it begins
the fresh blessing of sun filled mornings,
hedgerows fat with bluebells, wild garlic, buttercups
and the night's drift into dappled shadows.
The blue purple flash of swallows,
the busyness of the wren,
a fat bullfinch, and later,
a slender green one too.
The chestnut glow of horses coats,
the steady rhythm of kayak paddle,
of boat engine,
of farm machinery,
wafting across the bay,
coasting to Carningli,
disturbing crow, jackdaw, red kite and buzzard alike.

I walk past your house,
winter frozen and
ghosted after your death, some five years since,
and I glimpse you at your kitchen window,
ordering fish or a newspaper,
shooing out adders,
tending your garden.

But it's too late now to break the season's mood;
the light has stolen in,
and mussels lie on Newport beach
as perfect as an Old Master,
framed in sand and shell.

And all is well.
Yes, all is well.

Remembrance Sunday

What would you have had us remember
As you mustered in the trenches,
Around the gun emplacements?
As you hopped into the cockpit
And flung yourself skywards,
Or plumbed the depths
Submerged and submarined?
Should we remember your bravery?
Your mockery? Your cynicism in the face of duty?
Your gut wrenching anxiety,
Your fear, your mortal pain,
As you were killed and wounded,
Again and again and again?

Do the flags, the parades,
The preachers, the cavalcades,
Act as sufficient homage?
Or would peace, justice, equality
Be more deserving of your patronage?

But whichever,
It is true.
We must continue
To remember you.

A Confirmation Service

England - On the Eve of War

The sun streams through stained glass
While the United Nations
Remain at an impasse.

The saints gaze sympathetically
Upon the massed ranks
Of the well-to-do,
Whilst in the Azores
Various – mostly closing – diplomatic doors
Were slamming, presidentially.

The Bishop's deputy gave a pleasant homily
About joining the Bread of Life dining club
While many a distracted family
Were eagerly awaiting
Sunday lunch in a riverside pub.

The fashion sense at this august gathering
Left little to the imagination.
I was not aware that mink draped over the shoulder
Remained in style,
Only serving confirmation
That God, perhaps,
Maybe for a little while,
Had popped out of the building.

And amidst the prayers for peace and justice
The threat and tumult,
Of impending war,
As was
Is ever now.
Just is.

Two Rabbits – a poem on 9/11

Two rabbits,
oblivious to
two towers tumbling
and thousands of
subsequent oblivions.
Sometimes we forget
that telegraph poles
were once trees,
and that great civilisations,
and their emblems,
never lose their capacity to lose their dominion
and be brought,
awesomely, abruptly,
to their knees.
In the sands at Bournemouth
Someone has scraped a name –
Caitlyn.
I hope it was the work of a lover.
For we must remember
That love's constancy
aims to please.
Meantime,
we are all but as rabbits,
caught in the twin beams of headlights
and impending oblivion.

A poem for the Unknown Iraqi

- and for soldiers everywhere

The unknown Iraqi, anonymous, at least, to me,
lies sprawled and dead
and splayed across my TV screen.
Alone, forlorn, tattered,
The unspoken agony of the recently deceased.
His shoe is smudged with desert sand,
The socks, grey, thin and
Mouse-like feet.
Killed in action?
Killed in anger?
Killed in the frantic scramble – the near paralysis –
of impending defeat?
He is gone.
He is mute.
One end result of a game that's been played many
thousands of times,
A scene replayed across the ages,
As one "just" war (and its own war crimes)
concludes,
And recrimination rages.
War makes of peace a miser,
And the unknown Iraqi lies dead, and,
Unlike me, unlike us,
Cannot grow any older, and yet be
None the wiser.

Monty's gone

Rape seed golden glowing in this sunny bonus of a summer.
Ragwort flourishing likewise.
And the fields are fat with promise.

The train is full.
One man is sleeping.
A woman keeping watch over her young children.
The train manager is Spanish, his accent charming.
It's a Sunday morning, mid July,
And I am wondering why death
Is so disarming.

I am heading home, and somehow
That seems just so unfair.
These gifts of colour
Riot before my eyes.
The waft of fresh coffee,
A newspaper, a sandwich, spring water.
These seem such strangely held privileges right now
In the light of a friend's demise.
When, all too swiftly,
We are robbed of possibility.

Grief is etched, emblazoned in the sharpening sunlight.
As keenly honed as the tattoo I tried to read,
Blued on the arm of a man I passed at Victoria.

The coffee is hot, it burns my tongue,
Reminding me I am alive,
With memories to treasure.
For which I find myself both grateful
And yet perplexed,
In equal measure.

Yesterday, maybe even as you were slipping away from us,
The slivered breath of the final time,
The sun gorged the palette of the church's stained glass windows.
I left the shadowed stillness of that hallowed ground,
Having listened to the choir's final burst of joy sung as
'Something inside so strong'.
We all need that, I guess.

The sun still shone.
Cricket matches, cycle races, tennis tournaments
Went on.
Lost and won.

Festival goers basked in the midday sun.
But the globe span a little more slowly.
A shadow glimpsed, then it swiftly moved on.
Now that Monty's gone.
Monty's gone.

For Graham

Graham.
It's 105 days since I wanted to tell you that
I really liked your T shirt,
As you lay scared and hurting.
The nurses soothed your parched lips
Guided you to tiny sips
As you roared, swore, questioned our reality,
Convinced that we might be demons, or something worse,
Fell back, exhausted, a breath, a muttered curse.
At other points, emerging from the morphine fuelled depravity,
Seeing us there, those who loved you,
Son, lover, sister, brother, daughter, friend,
"Are you real?" you whispered, almost childlike
In your wonderment, "Oh, yes!"
And now you've left us,
To mourn your love of jazz, your intellect, your constant quest, your sardonic wit,
Even those last days of thundering, we miss.

There are Irish people singing on the train today.
Stars streamed the sky last night,
And I looked out for a shooting star that bore your name.
At Llangwm the Cleddau will caress your memory,
But now, your ship has sailed westward,
As we pass, as the living must, onward.

On Grief

The startling silence of grief.
The implosion of emotion.
Sadness, beyond belief.
Autumn leaves weeping onto the red brick building.

The Sun

The sun dips seawards,
Like a fattened calf to the slaughter.
I sip red wine
And dream
Of Mediterranean skies and times.

Taken from headstones in a Battersea graveyard

Entered the light.
Fell asleep.
At home with God.
Gone with the angels above.
Passed away.
Reunited.
One of God's best.
Entered into rest.
For ever with the Lord.
Weep not for me, but prepare to follow.

Gravestones, battered, broken, bruised.
Peace, ah, perfect peace.
The traffic noise, the siren calls, sometime soon
Will cease.

Springtime

I lay on my back imagining death
on the bridge that crosses our stream.
The moon framed by ivy,
A wisp of cigarette like cloud above,
Jackdaws, chaffinch, robins too.
The ravens like bombers.
The oak still budding.
The pine still sprouting.
Daffodils turned their heads towards the earth.
I stood up – spring, rebirth.

It might be;
Boston, Iraq, Syria, Tripoli
The trenches, Gettysburg, Gallipoli.
Roman official, Chinese sage, Ancient Greek,
21st century computer geek.

It might be;
Bhopal, Pompeii
Volcanic lava shake,
A 90 year old stuck in A and E,
An inconvenience of age, as opposed to an emergency.

Earthquake, Hitler, tsunami,
Stalinist purge victim,
Ghengis Khan casualty,
Or simply fallen foul of indifference.

I might be;
Baroness Thatcher,
Pomp and circumstance.
Or a shattered child in Libya,
Death unremarked,
A happenstance.
Died in 'friendly fire',
Or at terrorism's indiscriminate chance.

From death then, no escape,
But for now,
As the rain pushes up the darkening earth,
Nature's gift, a promise kept,
Rebirth, rebirth.
Joy to be alive,
And how!

September Song (#1) for you

A sunny September day,
The train has whisked me away
To do my duty
In search of booty.
Already the summer
Seems a ghost,
A whispered sunlit kiss,
A glimpse of bliss,
Now beached, becalmed and boat house stowed,
At most.
A friend died,
The oyster catchers cried,
Sandcastles were constructed,
Surfboards, golf clubs, wet suits were duly dusted off,
And winter's sullen cough was,
By sun-lightened lungs,
Abducted.
Other friends came and stayed,
House martins roosted,
Rabbit numbers were flagrantly boosted
As swallows caroused and played.
And wrens gave way to bullfinch.
And fruit, flower and grumbling vegetables
Were seeded, weeded,
Duly doused
And pies and sauces made.

The side swiped fields are fat with harvest promise now,
School, work and other such tyranny
Reels us in.
And though
Some such aspects might drain me,
Ultimately the song of summer
Remains, a snapshot in the mind,
A storehouse of gold, albeit in kind,
To warm, feed, sustain me.

September Song (#2) for you

Harvest gold fields fractured by
The cloud greyed green trees,
A small posse of piebald ponies,
Forlorn in the autumn mist and rain,
The train fleeing westward,
And me?
I am gladly
Homeward bound.

Snowfall over Newport

Snowflakes, fat and magical,
Falling fast upon our seaside town,
We hot foot it up onto Carningli,
Hiking at the odd angles
Which snow (and sand)
Demand.
Newport Bay lies below,
Muffled now, the silence of the snowstorm aftershock,
A swarm of starlings split the leadened sky,
The eerie wing beats of this huge flock
Mingle with tobogganists careering cries nearby.
Home, the windows glowing,
Chimney smoke signals our duskening guide
And still, as moonlit darkness hits its stride,
Stealthily, greedily, it is snowing.

Spring driven thing

It's a spring like day
And we are walking
Three dogs, you and I
In Pengelli woods
Marvelling at the cathedral of trees
Stepping through the quickening stems of wild
garlic and of bluebells, pushing up promises

There's a rough bench to rest on
And the chance to sit
Watching the stream slip by
Calling out its spring time song
Water music for the ear
Greened bark and worsened stone
Go gently on the eye

We talk, you're writing once more
A matter of delight
Whilst spring adopts its rites alike
We recommence our Sunday hike
Kicking up a storm of last year's leaf fall
Marshmallowed, moulded woodland floor
Winter slowly shrinking back
As the new season slides through the quietly
opening door.

At Sea

Passing Cape Horn,
I massage your back, and,
Nuzzling the back of your neck,
I drink in the smell of your sun streaked hair,
A scent in which I might happily drown.
The water around Cape Horn is deep,
Danger flooding its borders.
Meanwhile, I find myself,
Still steeped in the depths of you
And, as the waiter calls for orders,
And the sea retains a steel grey hue,
The boat begins to turn towards Tierra del Fuego
And the fire burns bright
At the bottom of the world.
And the flag I fly for you,
Is loose, unfettered and unfurled.
I'm wrapped around your neck
As we, at sea,
Sail around Cape Horn.

Epiphany

Alarmed, perhaps, by clarion bells,
The kingfisher lets fly
Its gift of jewels.
The morning sunlight slips
In sheets of fire,
Pillowing our morning bed.

The Three Kings have passed us by,
Somewhere between Bethlehem
And the South Tyrol.
But we have Venice once more
And the magical, moated, bird sparkled morning
instead.

A small poem about weather and feeling angry

The north easterly wind blew my anger
across the scuddy waved bay
as the dogs scampered
dolphin like
amongst the autumn dying bracken
and the cairn lay bare
blistered by the blasting gusts.

Down the hill I walked toward redemption
in the shelter of your lingering arms
recovering my humours
as I realised that I must.

and as if in homage to equilibrium restored
the gale receded, the estuary echoed to the
keening of oyster catchers
the slow calling of geese and gulls.

And a pink flushed sunset spoke to me
even amidst emotional spills
of the kindness of staying calm.

To conclude

Lost in translation?

Cooked Flan in Llandovery
I saw Steven in Llanstefan
And ate a pie in Pwyl
Sang Climb Every Mountain in Mwnt
And Angel Eyes on Carningli
Dined out in Dinas
Ate sewen in Fishguard
And eels in Llanelli
Bought a car in Cardiff
Saw a cygnet in Swansea
Got ripped off in Conway
Swam in Welshpool
Laughed in Laugherne
Got wrecked in Wrexham
Wept in Torvaen
Had a haircut in Aberaeron
Was wistful in Aberystwyth
Hysterical in Hermon
Took a drop in Newport
Or was it bathed in Trefdraeth
Took a boat from Newquay
Spent a decade in Tenby
Sang in Treorchy

Drove a Morris Minor in Magor
Felt glum in Merthyr
Decided Neath was enough
Barbecued in Skewen
Mistook Skokholm for Sweden
Got evicted
To England!

What (maybe) God (might) think of the World

"How odd,"
thought God,
"a programme about something
which many of them do not believe to be here,"
and switched to BBC 2
and poured a metaphysical pint of beer.
"Hmmm ... a curious mix of sceptics
and the very devout ...
and that young man, Vine?
whilst hardly divine, certainly seems devoted;
wonder how the punters voted?"
And so sat waiting for a sign.
"That's me,
on the TV,
all,
and nothing at all,
beginning and end,
a blessing, a curse,
and sometimes, in my name, (which is?)
something infinitely worse.
Bible,
Libel,
Koran,

Ashram,
hotel room reading,
and sometimes the trash can.
Prayers, prayers and more prayers,
heretics
and holy folk
eternally splitting hairs."
And so sat back, and wept a little for such cares.
"News? I've heard it all before.
Ought to show them the eternal door!
Always fretting over the Great Question.
Oh! Why, oh why?

Well, I'm not waiting
on all your debating.
The only advice I can give
humankind,
whether I may be,
do or do not live, is,
that you would be wise to keep me in mind."
And so sat up, and flipped channels to Sky.

and finally ... a tongue twister

There is,
perhaps,
precious little
to prevent Patrick
from protecting
his property properly.

www.ingramcontent.com/pod-product-compliance
Lightning Source LLC
Chambersburg PA
CBHW061456040426
42450CB00008B/1384